SEMINOLE
History and Culture

Helen Dwyer and D. L. Birchfield

Consultant Robert J. Conley
Sequoyah Distinguished Professor at Western Carolina University

Gareth Stevens
Publishing

Please visit our website, www.garethstevens.com. For a free color catalog of all our high-quality books, call toll free 1-800-542-2595 or fax 1-877-542-2596.

Library of Congress Cataloging-in-Publication Data

Dwyer, Helen.
Seminole history and culture / Helen Dwyer and D.L. Birchfield.
    p. cm. — (Native American library)
Includes index.
ISBN 978-1-4339-7430-4 (pbk.)
ISBN 978-1-4339-7431-1 (6-pack)
ISBN 978-1-4339-7429-8 (library binding)
1. Seminole Indians—History. 2. Seminole Indians—Social life and customs. I. Birchfield, D. L., 1948- II. Title.
E99.S28D94 2012
975.9004'973859—dc23

                        2011045568

New edition published in 2013 by
Gareth Stevens Publishing
111 East 14th Street, Suite 349
New York, NY 10003

First edition published 2005 by Gareth Stevens Publishing

Copyright © 2013 Gareth Stevens Publishing

Produced by Discovery Books
Project editor: Helen Dwyer
Designer and page production: Sabine Beaupré
Photo researchers: Tom Humphrey and Helen Dwyer
Maps: Stefan Chabluk

Photo credits: Corbis: pp. 8 (Lake County Museum), 11, 17 (top), 32 (Walter Bibikow); Getty Images: pp. 35 (Stephen Chernin/Stringer), 39 (Stephen Chernin/Stringer); Native Stock: pp. 10, 15 (bottom), 16, 17 (bottom), 18, 19, 21, 22, 23 (top), 24 (both), 25, 26 (both), 27, 31, 33, 34, 36, 38; Peter Newark's American Pictures: pp. 12, 20; North Wind Picture Archives: pp. 13, 14, 15 (top), 23 (bottom); Shutterstock.com: pp. 5 (Robert Fullerton), 37 (Henryk Sadura); Wikimedia: pp. 7, 28 (Rodney Cammauf/National Park Service), 29 (top) (Dcoetzee), 29 (bottom; Lori Oberhofer/National Park Service).

Printed in the United States of America

CPSIA compliance information: Batch #CS12GS: For further information contact Gareth Stevens, New York, New York at 1-800-542-2595.

CONTENTS

Words that appear in the glossary are printed in **boldface** type the first time they appear in the text.

INTRODUCTION

The Seminoles are a people of Oklahoma and Florida. They are just one of the many groups of Native Americans who live today in North America. There are well over five hundred Native American tribes in the United States and more than six hundred in Canada. At least three million people in North America consider themselves to be Native Americans. But who are Native Americans, and how do the Seminoles fit into the history of North America's native peoples?

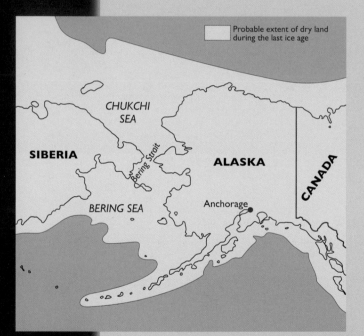

Probable extent of dry land during the last ice age

Siberia (Asia) and Alaska (North America) are today separated by an area of ocean named the Bering Strait. During the last ice age, the green area on this map was at times dry land. The Asian ancestors of the Seminoles walked from one continent to the other.

THE FIRST IMMIGRANTS

Native Americans are people whose **ancestors** settled in North America thousands of years ago. These ancestors probably came from eastern parts of Asia. Their **migrations** probably occurred during cold periods called **ice ages**. At these times, sea levels were much lower than they are now. The area between northeastern Asia and Alaska was dry land, so it was possible to walk between the continents.

Scientists are not sure when these migrations took place, but it must have been more than twelve thousand years ago. Around that time, water levels rose and covered the land between Asia and the Americas.

The Cliff Palace at Mesa Verde, Colorado, is the most spectacular example of Native American culture that survives today. It consists of more than 150 rooms and pits built around A.D. 1200 from sandstone blocks.

By around ten thousand years ago, the climate had warmed and was similar to conditions today. The first peoples in North America moved around the continent in small groups, hunting wild animals and collecting a wide variety of plant foods. Gradually these groups spread out and lost contact with each other. They developed separate **cultures** and adopted lifestyles that suited their **environments.**

SETTLING DOWN

Although many tribes continued to gather food and hunt or fish, some Native Americans began to live in settlements and grow crops. Their homes ranged from underground pit houses and huts of mud and thatch to dwellings in cliffs. By 3500 B.C., a plentiful supply of fish in the Pacific Ocean and in rivers had enabled people to settle in large coastal villages from Alaska to Washington State. In the deserts of Arizona more than two thousand years later, farmers constructed hundreds of miles of **irrigation** canals to carry water to their crops.

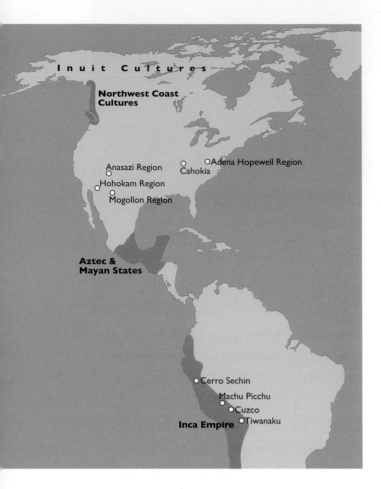

In the map:
Inuit Cultures
Northwest Coast Cultures
Anasazi Region
Hohokam Region
Mogollon Region
Adena Hopewell Region
Cahokia
Aztec & Mayan States
Cerro Sechin
Machu Picchu
Cuzco
Tiwanaku
Inca Empire

This map highlights some of the main early American cultures.

In the Ohio River valley between 700 B.C. and A.D. 500, people of the Adena and Hopewell cultures built clusters of large burial mounds, such as the Serpent Mound in Ohio, which survives today. The ancestors of the Seminoles were **mound builders** in Georgia and Alabama. In the Mississippi **floodplains**, the native peoples formed complex societies. They created mud and thatch temples on top of flat earth pyramids. Their largest town, Cahokia, in Illinois, contained more than one hundred mounds and may have been home to thirty thousand people.

CONTACT WITH EUROPEANS

Around A.D. 1500, European ships reached North America. The first explorers were the Spanish. Armed with guns and riding horses, they took over land and forced the Native Americans to work for them. The Spanish were followed by the British, Dutch, and French, who were looking for land to settle and for opportunities to trade.

When Native Americans met these Europeans, they came into contact with diseases, such as smallpox and measles, that they had never experienced before. At least one half of all Native Americans, and possibly many more than that, were unable to overcome these diseases and died.

Guns were also disastrous for Native Americans. At first, only the Europeans had guns, which enabled them to overcome native peoples in fights and battles. Eventually, Native Americans obtained guns and used them in conflicts with each other. Native American groups were also forced to take sides and fight in wars between the French and British.

Horses, too, had a big influence in Native American lifestyles, especially on the Great Plains. Some groups became horse breeders and traders. People were able to travel greater distances and began to hunt buffalo on horseback. Soon horses became central to Plains trade and social life.

Pressure from European settlement in the 1700s forced the ancestors of the Seminoles to move south from Georgia

Billy Bowlegs was a Seminole chief in the 1850s.

and Alabama into Florida, which was controlled by the Spanish. Most of them were Creeks (Muscogees), but some people from other tribes also migrated to northern Florida, where they made a living as farmers and ranchers. Around 1770, all these people became known as Seminoles. As the Seminoles moved south into wetter areas of Florida, they were forced to survive by hunting and fishing.

At the end of the 1700s, people of European descent began to migrate over the Appalachian Mountains, looking for new land to farm and exploit. By the middle of the nineteenth century, they had reached the west coast of North America. This expansion was disastrous for Native Americans.

RESERVATION LIFE

Many native peoples were pressured into moving onto **reservations** to the west. The biggest of these reservations later became the U.S. state of Oklahoma. Native Americans who tried to remain in their homelands were attacked and defeated. In 1830, the United States began a campaign to move the Seminoles from Florida to Oklahoma. This led to wars of resistance between 1832 and 1858. Most Seminoles were eventually forced to Oklahoma, but a few hundred of them never surrendered and remained in southern Florida and the **Everglades**.

New laws in the United States and Canada took away most of the control Native Americans had over their lives. They were expected to give up their cultures and adopt the ways and habits of white Americans. It became a crime to practice their traditional religions. Children were taken from their homes and placed in

boarding schools, where they were forbidden to speak their native languages.

Despite this **persecution**, many Native Americans clung to their cultures through the first half of the twentieth century. The Society of American Indians was founded in 1911, and its campaign for U.S. citizenship for Native Americans was successful in 1924. Other Native American organizations were formed to promote traditional cultures and to campaign politically for Native American rights.

Seminole children in Florida in the 1920s.

THE ROAD TO SELF-GOVERNMENT

Despite these campaigns, Native Americans on reservations endured poverty and very low standards of living. Many of them moved away to work and live in cities, where they hoped life would be better. In most cases, they found life just as difficult. They not only faced **discrimination** and **prejudice** but also could not compete successfully for jobs against more established ethnic groups.

In the 1970s, the American Indian Movement (AIM) organized large protests that attracted attention worldwide. They highlighted the problems of unemployment, discrimination, and poverty that Native Americans experienced in North America.

The AIM protests led to changes in policy. Some new laws protected the civil rights of Native Americans, while other laws allowed tribal governments to be formed. Today tribal governments have a wide range of powers. They operate large businesses and run their own schools and health care.

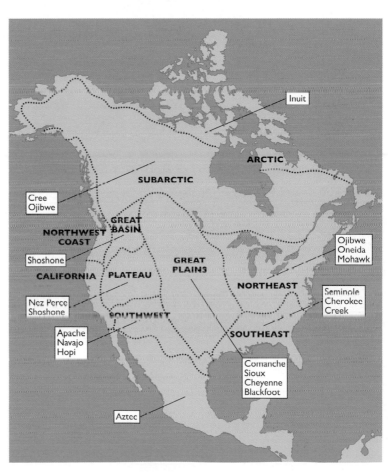

This map of North America highlights the main Native American cultural groups, along with the smaller groups, or tribes, featured in this series of books.

Chapter 1

LAND AND ORIGINS

A Florida Seminole man in traditional dress. This style of clothing was worn by Florida Seminoles from about 1700 to about 1830.

THE LAND OF THE SEMINOLES

The Seminoles are a North American native people who separated in the 1700s from a large **nation** of southeastern Indians called Muscogees (who are also known as Creeks). Their historic homelands include present-day Georgia and Alabama. Today, about ten thousand Seminoles live on four main reservations in Florida or in the Seminole Nation in Oklahoma.

ORIGIN STORY

Like many native cultures, the Seminoles have, for centuries, told a story to explain how they arrived on the continent. The Seminole origin story tells of a time, long ago, when the tribe emerged from a cave deep beneath the ground.

The Indian people now known as the Seminoles lived in Florida by the end of the eighteenth century.

They arrived in their homeland in the Southeast after a long journey from the West.

MOUND-BUILDING ANCESTORS

The Muscogees and Seminoles are descended from a great civilization of mound builders in the woodlands east of the Mississippi River. Today, state parks in Georgia and Alabama preserve some of those historic earthen mounds.

The Seminole people say that their name is a word in their own language meaning "a free people." Non-Seminoles have often assumed that the name comes from a Spanish word, *cimarron,* meaning "wild."

The Muskogean Language

Seminole is a Muskogean language, which is the great language family of the Southeast. The Muscogees (Creeks), Choctaws, Chickasaws, and many other smaller tribes speak languages from this family.

Seminole	Pronunciation	English
hokte	hoek-tee	woman
honvnwv	hoe-nun-wuh	man
hoktvce	hoek-tee	girl
cepvn	che-bon	boy
eccaswv	etch-a-sa-wa	beaver
acentv	a-chin-tuh	rattlesnake

The base of Monks Mound at Cahokia in Illinois is larger than the Great Pyramid's base in Egypt.

Chapter 2

HISTORY

LIFE IN THE NEW LAND

After the Spanish claimed Florida in 1585, European diseases and war between Spain and England wiped out the original Indian people of Florida. During the 1700s, Muscogees from present-day Georgia and Alabama began moving to that empty land in northern Florida, which was still Spanish territory. By 1775, they had formed a separate tribe in northern Florida, known as Seminoles.

The Seminoles enjoyed a good life as farmers and ranchers. Their population increased to about six thousand as small groups of Indians from other southeastern tribes joined them.

Runaway black slaves sought refuge among the Florida Seminoles. The former American slaves became important **allies** of the tribe.

SLAVES AND SEMINOLES

The Seminoles also welcomed the many African American slaves who ran away from the English colonies and joined them. Although some became slaves of the Seminoles, they were treated differently — and better — than slaves in the colonies. Others married Seminoles and became members of the tribe. Some former slaves even formed villages near the Seminoles and became farmers and cattle ranchers like the Seminoles.

The slave owners in Georgia, on the northern border of Florida, however, tried to recapture their

This painting portrays Seminoles in battle. The fighting occurred in 1817 near Fort Scott in Florida.

runaway slaves by invading Florida in the early 1800s. When the Seminoles resisted those efforts, war broke out between the Seminoles and the Georgians. In 1815, General Andrew Jackson helped the Georgians by ordering the U.S. Army to attack the Seminoles in Florida.

In 1819, Spain sold Florida to the United States, and in 1821, large numbers of Americans began moving to Florida under the protection of the U.S. Army. The Seminoles were forced to leave their farms and flee south. Once again, they were a people on the move, but this time they were leaving the rich farmland of northern Florida for a very different kind of environment in central and south Florida.

The Battle of Negro Fort

On July 27, 1816, a tragedy occurred in the war between the U.S. Army and the Seminoles for control of northern Florida. A U.S. gunboat sailed up the Apalachicola River to a Seminole fort and fired a cannonball that had been heated red hot in hopes of setting fire to the fort. It landed in the fort's gunpowder storage area and blew the whole place to pieces. In an instant, the explosion killed about three hundred African American men, women, and children and about thirty Seminoles.

LIFE IN THE SWAMPS

The land in central Florida was not as well suited to farming and cattle raising as northern Florida had been. The Seminoles had to change their way of life and rely more on hunting and fishing.

With some of the largest swamps on Earth, southern Florida was an even bigger change of environment. The Florida Everglades are a huge area of tall grass growing out of shallow water, with small islands hidden among the glades.

A Seminole village in the Everglades. The U.S. Army had great difficulty finding the Seminoles in the vastness of the Everglades.

THE SEMINOLE WARS

However, the Seminoles would not be allowed to live in peace in their new homes. In 1830, the United States passed the Indian Removal Act and demanded that all Seminoles leave Florida and move to the West. Some Seminoles signed the **Treaty** of Paynes Landing in 1832, and they were removed to Indian Territory (which later became Oklahoma).

Led by Osceola and Wildcat, however, some Seminoles refused to be removed — they went to war. The war lasted from 1835 to 1842 and became the costliest Indian war — in both money and men — in U.S. history. Many Seminoles were killed, and it cost the

This painting portrays the U.S. Army capturing Seminole chiefs during the Seminole wars.

United States more than $20 million and the lives of fifteen hundred U.S. soldiers. A few hundred Seminoles were able to hide in the swamps, until, finally, the army gave up trying to remove them.

Another Seminole war broke out in 1855, lasting until 1858, but again the U.S. Army was not able to defeat the Florida Seminoles. They would remain in Florida, separated from most of the tribe that was now in Indian Territory.

Osceola

Osceola (1804–38) became the most famous Seminole war chief in the war of 1835–42 in Florida. His leadership of the Seminoles in battle caused the U.S. Army great frustration and the loss of many men. Unable to defeat him, the army used **deceit** to capture him, seizing him when he attended a **negotiation** under a white flag of **truce** in 1837. He was sent to prison in South Carolina, where he died the following year.

Seminole chief Osceola showed his contempt for one U.S. treaty proposal by stabbing the paper with his knife.

The Trail of Tears. Seminoles suffered great hardships and many deaths during their forced removal from Florida to Indian Territory.

SEMINOLE REMOVAL: A TRAIL OF TEARS

The removal of the Seminoles and the other southeastern tribes (Choctaws, Muscogees, Chickasaws, and Cherokees) during the 1830s is one of the cruelest episodes in U.S. history. Their journey from Florida to Indian Territory is known as the "Trail of Tears" because so many native people died. The U.S. government did not provide adequate food, clothing, shelter, or medical supplies during the removal. Weakened by hunger and cold, the Seminoles fell victim to illness as they were moved north during the winter from the warm climate they were used to.

The Seminoles were not all forced from Florida at once. At first, only the Seminoles who had agreed to the removal treaty were removed. Later, during the war, other groups of Seminoles were removed as they were captured by the U.S. Army. Some Seminoles tried to avoid removal, and the warfare in Florida, by fleeing to Mexico. They became unhappy there, however, and within a few years, they joined their tribe in Indian Territory.

A black Seminole woman named Hannah in Florida in 1925. She was thought to have been about 105 years old at that time and the only living survivor of the Seminole wars of the nineteenth century.

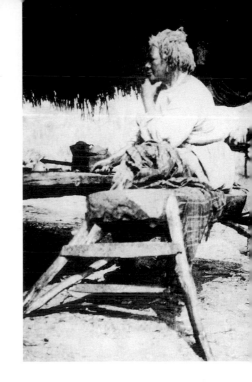

By the time the last Seminole war ended in 1858, most Seminoles had been removed from Florida. Only two or three hundred managed to avoid removal and stay in Florida.

SEMINOLES AFTER REMOVAL

The Seminoles who remained in Florida became a nearly forgotten people during the

Black Seminoles

The former African American slaves who had joined the Seminoles in Florida fought valiantly against the United States with their Seminole allies. In 1849, however, led by John Horse (also known as Juan Caballo), they fled to the border region of Mexico and Texas. Some of them joined the U.S. Army and became famous as the "Seminole Negro Scouts" under their leader, Sergeant John Kibbetts. After the American **Civil War**, many of them again served in the army. Today, many of their **descendants** live near Brackettville, Texas, near the border with Mexico.

An actor portraying a Seminole Negro scout. The black Seminole soldiers gained fame on the western frontier as scouts for the U.S. Army.

last half of the nineteenth century and for much of the twentieth century. They survived mostly by hunting and fishing in southern Florida in the Big Cypress Swamp, near Lake Okeechobee, or in the Everglades.

The U.S. government forced the Seminoles who were removed to Indian Territory to once again become a part of the Muscogee (Creek) Nation. Conditions in the Muscogee Nation after removal were horrible. The United States government failed to supply the food and farming equipment it had promised. The government officials who were supposed to provide the food stole the money and gave the Indians barrels of spoiled bacon instead.

THE CIVIL WAR TAKES A TOLL

The Seminoles suffered great hardship again during the American Civil War of 1861 to 1865, when armies from both sides plundered Indian Territory, raiding farms and stealing food and livestock. The war divided the Seminole people as it did the people of the United States. Seminole soldiers fought in both the **Union** and **Confederate** armies during the war.

Seminole men, women, and children after confinement to reservation life in Florida. Most Seminoles were removed to Indian Territory, but a few hundred were able to hide in the swamps and avoid removal.

An early photo of the Seminole town of Wewoka in Indian Territory. The Seminoles in Indian Territory watched helplessly as American settlers crowded in among them and eventually took away their land.

Finally, after the Civil War, the Seminoles in Indian Territory were allowed to separate from the Muscogees and form the Seminole Nation. They created a school system and became prosperous farmers, until non–native Americans once again began pouring into their lands in 1870s and 1880s, demanding Indian land for themselves.

When the state of Oklahoma was formed in 1907, the Seminoles were forced to become citizens of the new state and to give up their nation and all their land, except for small individual farms. In 1935, however, the Seminoles in Oklahoma were allowed to form a limited government. Finally, in the 1970s, they were allowed to adopt a **constitution** and form the Seminole Nation of Oklahoma, so they might govern themselves.

Wildcat

Wildcat (1810–57) was a famous Seminole war leader during the war of 1835 to 1842 in Florida. Captured with Osceola and sent to prison with him, Wildcat made a daring escape and continued fighting. When captured again, he was sent to Indian Territory in 1841. Unhappy with conditions there, he led his band of Seminoles to Mexico, where he died in 1857.

Chapter 3

TRADITIONAL WAY OF LIFE

TRADITIONAL CULTURE

Seminole culture is matrilineal, meaning that people's family tree is traced through the mother's line, rather than the father's as in European American culture. Seminole culture is also matrilocal, meaning that when a man and a woman get married, they live with the wife's extended family and the children are automatically members of the wife's **clan**.

These arrangements avoid many problems that are common in other cultures. First, spouse abuse is much less common because a wife is surrounded by her male relatives. Second, problems or

These Seminole women in Florida are making cornmeal. They remove the corn from the cob and then pound it into a coarse powder with a stick.

A young Seminole boy in traditional dress. Seminole women are proud of the skill it takes to make clothing like this.

uncertainties regarding child **custody** in the event of a divorce are also avoided. Because the children are members of the wife's clan, the children stay with the mother in the event of a divorce.

SEMINOLE UNCLES

Seminole children receive much of their training from their uncles, especially the brothers of their mother. The role of uncle is an important one in Seminole culture — uncles have more responsibility in raising a child than the parents. Parents are believed to be too emotionally close to their children to be able to see what might be best for a child. The children benefit greatly, surrounded by relatives who care about them very much.

Colorful Clothing

Seminole women have developed styles of clothing that are among the most distinctive of all the Indians in North America. They use patches of cloth, sewn together in strips of alternating color and pattern, to make shirts and dresses that are both striking and colorful. Grandmothers and mothers teach this craft to young Seminole girls, who take great pride in learning this very distinctive method of making clothing.

Seminole Watercraft

The Seminoles in Florida developed great skill in the art of building boats that were suited to their environment. For the shallow water of the Everglades, they fashioned a tree log into a long, narrow, lightweight craft. They propelled the craft by standing in the back of the boat and pushing it through the water with a long pole. For deep water, they hollowed out big logs with fires and made dugout canoes that they used to travel on the ocean, going as far as the islands of the Bahamas off Florida's eastern coast.

CHANGING ENVIRONMENT, CHANGING LIVES

The Seminole people have proven to be very adaptable to changing conditions and different environments. When they first settled in northern Florida, their lives were not much different from what they had been among the Muscogees. They planted fields of corn, beans, and squash, and they raised cattle, hunted, and fished.

When they were driven from northern to central and southern Florida, however, they found themselves in an environment not as well suited to agriculture or raising cattle. Even if the land had been more suitable to their former lifestyle, their cattle and their agricultural fields would have been easy targets for the large U.S. armies that hunted them.

The Seminoles survived by adapting to the vastness of the water-covered Everglades and the big swamps nearby. They learned how to harvest the edible plants in the new environment, learned how to depend more on fishing than on hunting, and learned how to find the small islands in the swamps where they could build their houses.

Chickee

The Seminole chickee is well suited to the environment of southern Florida. This style of house is built on a platform a few feet above the ground to protect it against flooding. An open-sided structure with no walls, the chickee allows cooling breezes to flow through the house. The roof is thatched with leaves from the palmetto plant, providing a deep, cool shade and protection from the rain. The structure can be built quickly, from materials readily at hand.

The Everglades' environment made it very difficult and very costly for the U.S. Army to find the Seminoles. They became very skilled at laying **ambushes** for the soldiers, blending into the vegetation until it was too late for the soldiers to realize they had entered a trap.

The environment also made it more difficult for the Seminoles to carry on their traditional form of government, which had been organized into villages. In the swamps, the people had to become more scattered, living in extended family groups much smaller than their former villages and relying on the leadership of the family **elders**.

These Seminoles are transporting lumber into the Everglades. The lumber was salvaged from a shipwreck on a nearby ocean beach.

Stickball is still played today. These modern Seminoles are playing stickball at the Big Cypress Reservation in Florida.

SEMINOLE SPORTS AND GAMES

The Seminoles are so well known in history for the Seminole wars — and for the fact that they are the only Indian tribe that the United States went to war against but was unable to defeat — that they have gained an image as a warlike people. That image does not accurately portray the richness of Seminole life and the true character of the Seminole people, which can be seen in the tremendous importance they place on sports and games.

A Seminole Story

Seminoles love telling stories about the animal world. One story tells about a great ball game that was played by the birds against the four-footed animals. However, no one could decide which team the bat should be on, and at first both teams rejected this flying mammal. After much debate, the four-footed animals allowed the bat to play for them. In the game, the bat led the four-footed animals to a great victory.

Like all the southern Indians, and like many other Indians on the continent, Seminoles loved the game of stickball, which European Americans adopted, calling it lacrosse. The game is still played today but not on the scale of former days.

The big stickball games, called "match games," in which men competed against men, were events that held the entire tribe spellbound, with village competing against village in a frenzied effort that made a lasting impression on all outsiders who witnessed it. Often, the people would bet nearly all of their worldly possessions on a game of ball. Women and men of all ages competed together in other stickball games.

AN ACTIVE PEOPLE

The Seminoles had many other leisure activities and games, including the hoop and pole game, where one person rolled a hoop and the other person tried to hit it with a spear. Footraces were also very popular. They provided **endurance** training for the children and were a way for men and women to stay in good physical condition.

Today, Seminoles still place great value on **rigorous** athletic activity. Their sports teams for both men and women, particularly softball, play with great enthusiasm and skill.

SEMINOLE BELIEFS

After several centuries of attempts to suppress them by outsiders and the U.S. government, traditional Seminole religious beliefs and

A young Seminole boy competes at archery. With such weapons, the Seminole warriors were able to remain undefeated by the U.S. Army during the nineteenth century.

This traditional Seminole medicine man is carrying a gourd rattle in his right hand, an ancient part of ceremonial **rituals**.

On a Seminole reservation in Florida, a Seminole sells ingredients for traditional Seminole medical remedies.

worldview remain strong. From the Seminole viewpoint, humans are merely one of the many creatures on Earth, and all creatures have dignity and a spirit that must be respected. Traditional Seminoles try to live in harmony with the natural world. Many of their beliefs come from traditional stories, and many of those stories tell lessons about how to live in the world that they have learned from various animals.

Seminole religious and cultural beliefs are rich with stories of animals and humans sharing the world together and having an influence on each others' lives. It's not possible to understand how Seminoles view the world and their place in it without long exposure to the stories and the lessons they teach.

Seminoles and many other Indian tribes are not particularly interested in whether or not outsiders understand their religions. Many

Indians regard inquires about their religions as unwelcome questions about their personal and private lives because most Indian religions do not attempt to convert other people to their beliefs.

MEDICINE MEN

Medicine men continue to be important in Seminole life. They possess detailed knowledge of the healing powers of herbs and other remedies and carefully preserve the knowledge of magic formulas and ceremonies that the people rely upon to maintain both their health and their sense of well-being in the world.

The most important religious event is the annual Green Corn Ceremony. This event lasts four days in Oklahoma and seven days in Florida, in late June or July, when Seminoles camp together, play ball, and participate in dances, feasts, and religious rituals.

This woman is performing the Fancy Shawl Dance at the Seminole Tribal Fair Powwow.

Grave Houses

Many Seminoles continue the cultural tradition of covering a grave with a small grave house. The grave houses are about 3 feet (1 meter) high and about 6 feet (2 m) long. The sides of the houses look somewhat like a picket fence. They are found in Seminole cemeteries near the towns of Wewoka and Seminole in Oklahoma.

Seminole Origins

ANIMAL BEGINNINGS

In the Seminole origin story, the Creator made Earth. Then, very carefully, he created and shaped many animals to live on Earth. When he was satisfied that he had made enough different creatures, the Creator put them all in large shell, next to a young tree. As the tree grew, it wound its roots around the shell, and eventually the pressure of the roots cracked the shell. The Wind blew around the shell, giving the animals breath and helping them to break free. The creatures all searched for suitable places to live. The Creator saw

The Florida panther is a rare sort of cougar. When the Seminole first told their origin story, this large cat was common in the Everglades and all over southern Florida. Today there are only around 120 of them left.

how they adopted many different lifestyles before he gave them names. His favorite of them all was the one he named Panther.

THE FIRST PEOPLE

Then the Creator began to make people and put them in a cave under the ground. When he had finished, he made the ground shake, and the cave burst open. The people found themselves surrounded by a thick fog. Completely lost, they staggered around in small groups until the Wind blew away the fog.

How the Clans Formed

At first the people knew nothing. Each group was helped by one of the animals, who taught them how to behave and survive. Finally, the Creator decided that each group of people should take the name of the animal that helped them. The first group to escape the fog and see the Wind became the Wind Clan. The people of the Panther Clan were especially favored by the Creator and became the lawmakers and medicine men.

From birth, children became members of their mother's clan. Over time, some clans died out. Today the Seminole Tribe of Florida has only eight clans.

The Deer Clan is named for the white-tailed deer, a very widespread mammal in the United States. In Florida, it is preyed upon by the Florida panther.

The Alligator Clan was named for the American alligator, which in this photo is fighting with a python. There are now more than a million of these alligators in Florida, but the Seminole Alligator Clan is extinct.

Chapter 4

SEMINOLE LIFE TODAY

THE SEMINOLE TRIBE OF FLORIDA

The U.S. government formally recognized the Seminole Tribe of Florida as a separate Indian tribe in 1957. Today, members of the tribe number about three thousand and occupy six reservations.

At 42,730 acres (17,300 hectares), Big Cypress Reservation is the largest of the federal reservations and is located on the northeastern edge of the Big Cypress Swamp in southern Florida. The Brighton Reservation has 35,800 acres (14,500 ha) and is located northwest of Lake Okeechobee. The Seminole (or Hollywood) Reservation near the city of Miami has only 480 acres (195 ha). The Tampa and Immokalee Reservations were established in 1979, followed by Fort Pierce in 1996, which has approximately fifty residents of mixed Seminole and African American ancestry.

This map shows the locations of the main Seminole reservations in southern Florida.

THE MICCOSUKEE TRIBE OF INDIANS OF FLORIDA

The Miccosukee Reservation was created in 1962, when the Miccosukee Tribe of Indians of Florida gained recognition by the U.S. government as a separate tribe. About four hundred Seminoles live on the Miccosukee Reservation, located in the Everglades about 25 miles (40 kilometers) west of Miami, close to the Big Cypress Reservation. Indians from more than forty tribes attend their Florida Annual

30

This Seminole farmer is harvesting sugarcane on the Big Cypress Reservation in Florida.

Indian Arts Festival each winter, which features dancing, singing, and exhibits of arts and crafts.

GOVERNING THE RESERVATIONS

Each of the reservations in Florida is governed by its own elected **council**. Those councils meet as a group each year at the Green Corn Ceremony. The councils have created tribal business activities, including tobacco shops, several **casinos**, campgrounds, citrus fruit groves, and cattle-ranching operations.

SEMINOLE TELEVISION

There are four cable television stations serving the Hollywood, Big Cypress, Brighton, and Immokalee Reservations. They are parts of the Seminole Broadcasting Department, which is funded by the tribe. The stations cover local events on the reservations, while the Broadcasting Department produces programs on Seminole culture and history, and covers tribal events and news. It also makes commercials and creates videos for the tribal government as well as for private customers.

HOMES, SCHOOLS, AND LAND

Since the last half of the twentieth century, many Seminoles have preferred modern housing to the traditional chickee. With profits from their casinos, they have built many new houses, schools for their children, and community centers and health-care facilities for the tribe.

One of the biggest projects is the Veterans' Building that opened in 2007 in Okeechobee. It is an impressive limestone building shaped like a five-pointed star to represent the five branches of the U.S. armed forces. Inside is

Students in the computer room in the successful Ahfachkee School on the Big Cypress Reservation.

an auditorium that seats more than five hundred people.

The tribal government's biggest concern is trying to acquire more land for their people while continuing to improve their quality of life.

EDUCATIONAL TOURISM

The Big Cypress Reservation houses the Billie Swamp Safari in the Everglades, where visitors can take an airboat or swamp buggy ride to see the wildlife.

The reservation's other big tourist attraction is the Ah-Tah-Thi-Ki Museum, which shows how the Seminoles used to live in the swamps of Florida. It also features a boardwalk leading to a re-created village and ceremonial grounds. Seminoles on the Hollywood and Miccosukee Reservations have also recreated traditional villages that give visitors a taste of Seminole lifestyles and crafts.

Tourists take the airboat through the swamps, part of the Billie Swamp Safari on the Big Cypress Reservation.

Alligator Wrestling

Seminoles in Florida have become famous for entertaining tourists by wrestling the large Florida alligators at small, roadside entertainment centers and at exhibitions on the reservations. Seminoles at the Miccosukee Reservation are particularly well known for their skill in wrestling the large, dangerous creatures. The alligators are not harmed, and the Seminole wrestlers are rarely injured.

Alligator wrestling on the Miccosukee Reservation in Florida. The Seminole alligator wrestlers are a popular tourist attraction and a source of tourist money for the tribe.

SEMINOLES TODAY IN OKLAHOMA

Today, there are about seven thousand members of the Seminole Nation of Oklahoma. The capital of their nation is located in Wewoka, Oklahoma.

The Seminoles govern themselves with an elected tribal council made up of two members from each of the tribe's fourteen bands. They operate tribal businesses, including tobacco shops that do not have to pay Oklahoma state taxes. They provide educational programs for their children, health-care programs for the tribe, and community centers that give tribal members a place to meet and socialize. One of their more recent programs is to encourage more people to learn the Seminole language.

The tribe's most important goal is to keep its tribal sovereignty, which is the right of the tribe to govern itself. To do this, tribal members must be aware of changes in how the U.S. government is handling Indian affairs. They must also guard against state officials who might wish to take away the independence of Indian tribes in Oklahoma.

AN OIL-RICH LAND

The Seminoles in Oklahoma should be among the wealthiest Indian tribes in the United States since it was on their land that the great Oklahoma oil boom took place in the early decades of the twentieth century.

A map of the Seminole Nation in Oklahoma.

However, most Seminoles were cheated out of their land by **corrupt** politicians, lawyers, and judges. The **fraud** took place on a huge scale, and the Seminoles were helpless to do anything about it. Now many Seminoles live near the poverty level.

CRAFT SKILLS

The Seminoles have provided an outlet for their artists and craftspeople to sell their

Seminole basket making, which requires great skill, is a craft handed down from generation to generation.

products at the Seminole Nation Museum in Wewoka. There, Seminole women display the high level of skill required in making their distinctive patchwork clothing, while men skilled at making the sticks used in stickball games offer them for sale. The sticks are made of slender, finely crafted pieces of hickory.

Seminole Patchwork

The tradition of making clothing from patchwork only began at the end of the nineteenth century, when there was a shortage of cloth. Seminole women began to sew together long, narrow strips of different cloths, either recycled from old clothing or from the ends of cloth rolls. In the early twentieth century, they began to use sewing machines, which made the work much quicker. As well as making their own clothes, they began to sell them to tourists. Now patchwork clothes are usually worn for special occasions. Women wear full, floor-length skirts, while men wear short patchwork jackets.

At this public gathering, many of the women have chosen to wear traditional patchwork dresses.

Seminole Nation Days

Seminole Nation Days, an annual celebration of Seminole culture in Oklahoma, is held each year in September in Seminole, Oklahoma. The event features Seminole arts and crafts, lots of food, visiting with old friends, and traditional Seminole dancing. Many Seminoles who now live outside the Seminole Nation in east-central Oklahoma plan their vacation around the event. Thus, it serves as a homecoming each year for many members of the tribe.

CONTEMPORARY SEMINOLE LEADERS

Seminoles have produced many famous artists and leaders who have attained distinction in their **professions**. Seminole journalist and tribal leader Betty Mae Tiger Jumper (1923–2011) became the first woman elected to lead the tribal council for the Seminole Nation of Florida in 1967. In 1949, she had been the first Florida Seminole to graduate from high school. She founded a newspaper for the tribe in 1963 and became its editor. In 1997, the Native American Journalists Association honored her with its Lifetime Achievement Award.

Led by a medicine man, these Seminole young people are preparing to perform a Stomp Dance.

Donald Fixico, born in 1951, is a Seminole who has achieved distinction as a professor of history, teaching at universities throughout the United States, and as director of the **Indigenous** Studies Program at the University of Kansas. He has published many books.

Jerome Tiger (1941–67), a Muscogee Seminole raised in Oklahoma, is among the most famous Indian artists. His paintings portray events ranging from the Green Corn Ceremony, to the Trail of Tears, to contemporary Indian life. Seminoles have produced many other leaders, including sculptor Kelly Haney. He has been a leader of the Oklahoma State Senate for many years.

The Oklahoma Capitol Dome

Oklahoma recently placed a dome on top of the state **capitol** building in Oklahoma City. The state commissioned Seminole sculptor Kelly Haney to create a large sculpture of an American Indian to put on top of the dome. Haney's sculpture is a Plains Indian warrior, ready for battle. The warrior's foot is tied to the ground, signifying that the warrior will not retreat. The statue was placed on top of the dome in the summer of 2002.

The new Oklahoma capitol dome with Kelly Haney's sculpture at the top.

Chapter 5

CURRENT SEMINOLE ISSUES

POLLUTION OF THE EVERGLADES

In the early twenty-first century, the main concern of the Miccosukee Seminoles in Florida has been the worsening pollution of the Everglades swamps where they live. The main pollutants are fertilizers and pesticides that are used in farming and eventually enter the swamps. The Miccosukees have filed several lawsuits in an attempt to make the Environmental Protection Agency and the South Florida Water Management District clean up the water.

Buffalo Tiger, a former chief of the Miccosukee Seminoles, is a leader in the campaign to clean up the swamps.

Nothing grows here anymore. We lived off the Everglades and we can't do that now. But if things keep going like this, when our young people grow up they won't have anything left. We used to hunt big fish, small fish so easy. And we'd eat them. Today I would never eat a fish again. Too much poison. We cannot drink the water, so people start eating fast food and getting fat and unhealthy.

Buffalo Tiger of the Miccosukee Seminoles, born in the Everglades in 1920

Members of the Seminole Tribe of Florida celebrate the purchase of the Hard Rock Cafe chain.

HARD ROCK AND MONEY PROBLEMS

In 2007, the Seminole Tribe of Florida bought the international Hard Rock Cafe chain of restaurants. The deal included more than one hundred cafes, several hotels, two casinos, and two concert venues. Profits from these, and from the tribe's casinos, mean that all tribe members receive regular payouts. Since 2003, however, several tribal leaders have been forced to resign after investigations have shown that they used large sums of tribal money for themselves and their families.

SEMINOLE FREEDMEN

For several years, the Seminole Freedmen in Oklahoma, who are the descendants of black Seminoles living in the 1800s, had claimed that they were full citizens of the Seminole Nation of Oklahoma. However, the tribal government had refused to allow them to receive the financial advantages of being tribal members. This finally changed in 2004, and the Freedmen were allowed the same rights as other Seminoles.

THE SEMINOLES' FUTURE

As the Seminoles look to the future, they now have the advantage of being allowed to govern themselves. They now have a voice in their own destiny, and that is a big change from the recent past.

TIMELINE

1540s	Spanish expedition of Hernando de Soto through Southeast.
early 1700s	European diseases and armies wipe out Florida Indians.
1700s	Muscogees (Creeks) who will become Seminoles move south into northern Florida; they are joined by runaway slaves; Seminole tribe is formed.
early 1800s	Georgia slave owners invade northern Florida trying to recapture their runaway slaves.
1815	Many Muscogees who had been defeated by the United States in the War of 1812 flee to the Florida Seminoles; General Andrew Jackson attacks the Seminoles in Florida.
1816	U.S. gunboat fires a red-hot cannonball at a Seminole fort on the Apalachicola River, causing a gunpowder store to explode, killing more than three hundred African Americans and Seminoles.
1819	Spain sells Florida to the United States.
1821	American settlers begin pouring into Florida, driving the Seminoles to the south.
1830	Congress passes Indian Removal Act, allowing the U.S. government to move Indians from their lands in the East to the West.
1832	Seminole removal treaty; many Seminoles are removed to Indian Territory (now Oklahoma).
1835–42	Seminole war in Florida between the United States and Seminoles who refuse to leave.
1849	Black Seminoles (former slaves) flee to Mexico and Texas.

1855–58	Last Seminole war in Florida; United States gives up trying to remove all Seminoles, leaving two or three hundred in Florida.
1861–65	U.S. Civil War devastates Seminoles in Indian Territory.
1880–90s	Seminoles in Indian Territory are forced to accept individual farms; most of their land is thrown open to white settlement.
1907	Seminole Nation is dissolved when Oklahoma becomes a state.
early 1900s	Seminoles do not benefit from oil boom in their homeland.
1935	Seminoles in Oklahoma form a limited government.
1957	Seminole Nation of Florida is formed, gains federal recognition.
1962	Miccosukee Indian Tribe of Florida gains federal recognition.
1970s	Seminoles in Oklahoma found new Seminole Nation.
1979	Seminoles open the first tribally operated casino in the United States in Hollywood, Florida. Immokalee and Tampa Reservations are established.
1980–90s	Tribal businessses help provide tribal revenue and programs.
1992	Seminoles in Florida and Oklahoma collect land claims against the United States. Independent Seminoles refuse to settle.
1996	Fort Pierce Reservation established in Florida.
2002	Seminole sculptor Kelly Haney's statue of an Indian warrior is placed on the new dome of the capitol building in Oklahoma City.
2006	Seminole Tribe of Florida purchases Hard Rock Cafe chain of restaurants.
2007	Veterans' Building opens in Okeechobee, Florida.
2011	Former Seminole tribal leader Betty Mae Tiger Jumper dies.

GLOSSARY

allies: groups who agree to work together for a common goal.

ambush: to capture or kill by trapping or lying in wait.

ancestor: a person from whom an individual or group is descended.

boarding schools: places where students must live at the school.

capitol: a building where a group of representatives meet to make laws.

casinos: buildings that have slot machines, card games, and other gambling games.

Civil War: the war between Northern and Southern U.S. states that lasted from 1861 to 1865.

clan: a group of related families.

Confederate: usually Southerners, the side that fought the federal government during the Civil War and tried to split the United States into two separate nations.

constitution: the basic laws and principles of a nation that outline the powers of the government and the rights of the people.

corrupt: acting dishonestly for money and personal gain.

council: a group of people who meet regularly to discuss issues or manage something.

culture: the arts, beliefs, and customs that make up a people's way of life.

custody: the care and keeping of a person or thing.

deceit: a dishonest act.

descendants: all the children and children's children of an individual or group; those who come after.

discrimination: unjust treatment usually because of a person's race or sex.

elder: an older person.

endurance: the ability to do something for a long time.

environment: objects and conditions all around that affect living things and communities.

Everglades: area of marshland or swamp, often under water and covered with tall grasses.

floodplain: the area of land beside a river or stream that is covered with water during a flood.

fraud: an act of tricking or cheating.

ice age: a period of time when the earth is very cold and lots of water in the oceans turns to ice.

indigenous: originating in a particular country or region.

irrigation: any system for watering the land to grow plants.

medicine men: religious leaders and healers.

migration: movement from one place to another.

mound builders: Indians in North America who built large earthen mounds for ceremonies, burials, and temples; ancestors of the Seminoles.

nation: people who have their own customs, laws, and land separate from other nations or peoples.

negotiation: talking to try to come to an agreement about differences.

persecution: treating someone or a certain group of people badly over a period of time.

prejudice: dislike or injustice that is not based on reason or experience.

professions: jobs that require lots of training and qualifications.

reservation: land set aside by the U.S. government for specific Native American tribes to live on.

rigorous: physically demanding.

rituals: systems of special ceremonies, usually spiritual ones.

stickball: a ball game played with a stick and a ball about the size of a tennis ball.

treaty: an agreement among two or more peoples or nations.

truce: a short stop in fighting to allow both sides to try to come to a peaceful agreement.

Union: usually Northerners, the side that stayed loyal to the federal government during the Civil War.

MORE RESOURCES

WEBSITES:

http://www.abfla.com/1tocf/seminole/semart.html
An illustrated article about Seminole patchwork.

http://www.bigorrin.org/seminole_kids.htm
Online Seminole Indian Fact Sheet for Kids in question-and-answer form with useful links.

http://www.kellyhaney.com/
The website of the Seminole sculptor Kelly Haney.

http://www.kennethjohnson.com/index.html
The website of the Seminole metalsmith Kenneth Johnson.

http://www.miccosukee.com/tribe.htm
The official site of the Miccosukee Tribe of Indians of Florida.

http://www.native-languages.org/seminole.htm#language
Numerous links to pages about the Seminole language, culture, and history.

http://www.semtribe.com
The official site for the Seminole Tribe of Florida.

http://www.semtribe.com/Culture/Art.aspx
Paintings by the Seminole artist Noah Billie.

http://www.seminolenation.com
The official site for the Seminole Nation of Oklahoma.

http://www.floridamemory.com/PhotographicCollection
Type the words "Seminole Indian" into this site's search engine and find hundreds of photos on Seminole life in Florida.

DVD:

Black Indians: An American Story. Rich-Heape Films, 2004.

BOOKS:

Annino, Jan Godown. *She Sang Promise: The Story of Betty Mae Jumper, Seminole Tribal Leader.* National Geographic Children's Books, 2010.

Brown, Virginia Pounds, and Laurella Owens. *The World of the Southern Indians: Tribes, Leaders, and Customs from Prehistoric Times to the Present.* NewSouth Books, 2011.

Downs, Dorothy. *Patchwork: Seminole and Miccosukee Art and Activities.* Pineapple Press, 2005.

Englar, Mary. *The Seminole: The First People of Florida.* Capstone Press, 2006.

Frank, Andrew K. *The Seminole (History & Culture of Native Americans).* Chelsea House Publications, 2010.

Gibson, Karen Bush. *Native American History for Kids: With 21 Activities.* Chicago Review Press, 2010.

King, David C. *First People.* DK Children, 2008.

King, David C. *The Seminole (First Americans).* Benchmark Books, 2006.

Koestler-Grack, Rachel A. *Osceola, 1804–1838 (American Indian Biographies).* Blue Earth Books, 2002.

Lund, Bill. *The Seminole Indians (Native Peoples).* Capstone Press, 2006.

Murdoch, David S. *North American Indian (DK Eyewitness Books).* DK Children, 2005.

Raffa, Edwina, and Annelie Rigsby. *Escape to the Everglades (Florida Historical Fiction for Youth).* Pineapple Press, 2006.

Tingle, Tim. *Spirits Dark and Light: Supernatural Tales from the Five Civilized Tribes.* August House, 2006.

Wilcox, Charlotte. *The Seminoles (Native American Histories).* Lerner Classroom, 2007.

THINGS TO THINK ABOUT AND DO

DIFFERENT KINDS OF HOMES

Can you draw pictures of a log cabin and a Seminole chickee to show the differences in the two kinds of houses?

A NEW LIFE

Imagine being moved from the swampland of Florida to the thickly wooded hills of Indian Territory. How would life be different? How would you adjust to the new surroundings? What new skills would you need to learn? Write an essay on what you imagine life would be like.

THE FEW AGAINST THE MANY

Can you think of some reasons why a small group of Indians in the swamps could hold out against a large army that was trying to capture them? Explain your thinking in a few paragraphs.

INDEX